# The Sa

Written by Chris Lutrario
Photographed by Robert Pickett

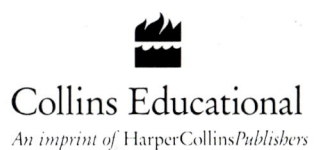

Collins Educational
*An imprint of* HarperCollins*Publishers*

Get two slices of bread.

Spread some butter on the bread.

Put some cheese
on the bread.

Put some tomato
on the cheese.

Put a slice of bread on top.

Eat it!

bread 　　　cheese

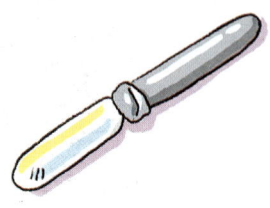

knife 　　　butter

tomato 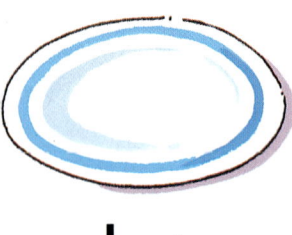　　　plate